JAZZ LEGENDS ALPHABET

Words by Robin Feiner

A is for **A**rt Blakey. The legendary drummer behind the classic song, Moanin', was an expert soloist with a keen ear for rhythm and tone. While playing with all-time greats like Monk and Charlie Parker, his experimental swing technique helped introduce a newer 'hard bop' style to jazz.

Bb

B is for Billie Holiday.
Lady Day sang with gripping,
raw emotion. As a civil rights
activist, she was known for
moving fans to tears through
songs like Strange Fruit and
Solitude. Long after her
passing, her soft, soothing
voice continues to win
hearts and minds.

C is for Chet Baker. With slower tempos, a relaxed nature, and his signature fedora, the 'Prince of Cool' gave a face to '50s West Coast Jazz. Although he also sang, fans remember him fondly as possibly the greatest trumpeter who ever lived, and a real hepcat.

D is for **D**ave Brubeck. Few knew their way around the keys like the 'Ambassador of Cool.' The Dave Brubeck Quartet released the iconic Time Out album in 1959. Take Five, from that album, with its catchy 5/4 rhythm, is the greatest-selling jazz single ever.

E is for Duke **E**llington. This legendary pianist and composer took up piano at the age of seven, leading to an epic career that spanned decades. Duke compiled hundreds of classic jazz standards, and some experts believe that he's the one who gave American music its own distinctive sound.

F is for **F**rank Sinatra. With timeless classics like Come Fly with Me and My Way, 'Ol' Blue Eyes' crooned his way through the '40s and '50s. He could make every song his own while making the ladies swoon. But he'll be best remembered as an entertainer with style and charisma.

G is for Benny **G**oodman. The 'King of Swing' was a talented clarinet player, as well as a key figure in the 1930s civil rights movement. He became the first white band leader in America to hire a Black musician, breaking segregation law. This act cemented Goodman as a true jazz legend.

H is for **H**erbie Hancock.
As an 11-year-old prodigy,
this jazz legend was already
playing Mozart with the
world-famous Chicago
Symphony Orchestra. But
with the funky, electronic
tones he made famous in
Watermelon Man, Hancock
created a new and influential
sound: jazz-funk-rock fusion.

I is for Illinois Jacquet. In the early '40s, very few brought down the house like Jean-Baptiste 'Illinois' Jacquet. With his rambunctious saxophone solos, he made the jazz world sit up and take notice. Loud and wild, his style is believed to have influenced R&B, Rock 'n' Roll, and the Blues.

J is for John Coltrane.
No one has ever made
magic with a saxophone
quite like 'Trane' — a nick-
name given to him by fellow
jazz legend Miles Davis.
He created Blue Train, A Love
Supreme, and Giant Steps,
iconic albums rich with his
gift for improv and
spirited rhythm.

K is for Gene **K**rupa. With his solo on Benny Goodman's Sing, Sing, Sing, this legend helped make drummers a staple in jazz bands. A Grammy Hall of Fame Inductee, he's a worthy rival to Buddy Rich, and was once called the 'Founding Father of the Modern Drumset.'

L is for Louis Armstrong. With his emotional solos and smooth vocal improvisation, the trumpeter and singer known as 'Pops' changed the face of jazz. His enthusiasm never wavered, even in the face of racism. With his angelic yet gravelly voice, he proved that it truly is a wonderful world.

M is for **M**iles Davis. 'The Prince of Darkness' changed the history of jazz and blues. In the '50s, he helped invent cool jazz and hard bop. In the '60s, he fused his orchestral jazz sound with Spanish rhythms. Davis will forever be celebrated as one of history's greatest musicians.

N is for Nina Simone. With her husky voice, the 'High Priestess of Soul' is considered one of the most influential jazz artists of the 20th century. Mississippi Goddam, To Be Young, Gifted and Black, and Four Women—these legendary Simone tracks became anthems of the civil rights movement.

O is for Oscar Peterson. Playing the piano with terrific speed and accuracy, Peterson is one of the finest musicians Canada has ever produced. 'The man with four hands' won eight Grammys, and played alongside Ella Fitzgerald, Louis Armstrong, and Billie Holiday.

P is for Charlie Parker. 'Bird' was famous in jazz circles for how hard he worked. He practiced the sax more than 15 hours a day, applying himself to fast tempos and unique harmonies. He was an ideas man, the composer of the famed Yardbird Suite, and an all-out jazz virtuoso.

Q is for 'Queen of Jazz' Ella Fitzgerald. With her pure, powerful voice, it's no wonder Ella became the first Black woman to win a Grammy. She was also a Presidential Medal of Freedom recipient. As Bing Crosby once said, 'Man, woman, or child, Ella's the greatest of them all.'

R is for Django **R**einhardt. After badly injuring his left hand as a teen, this legend had only his love of jazz and his index and middle finger to keep him going. Django developed the innovative, bohemian music style known as Manouche jazz.

S is for **S**tan Getz.
This legendarily smooth saxophonist reinterpreted The Girl from Ipanema, making it an international sensation. Alongside João Gilberto, he released the instant classic Getz/Gilberto album, popularizing bossa nova music.

T is for **T**helonious Monk. 'Melodious' once said, 'The piano ain't got no wrong notes.' So, he used them all with his innovative 'angular' style. It's that style that led to jazz standards like Round Midnight and Blue Monk. No wonder he's considered one of the greatest composers of all time.

U is for James 'Blood' Ulmer. Blood rose to fame in the '70s and '80s after playing with the likes of Art Blakey and Ornette Coleman. Tired of the same old sounds, he crafted his own, fusing jazz with Jimi Hendrix's style and techniques.

V is for Sarah **V**aughan. After winning a talent competition at the historic Apollo Theater, Sarah became a star at just 18 years old. She opened for Ella Fitzgerald the following week, toured with Dizzy Gillespie the following year, and soon became a jazz legend the world would never forget.

Ww

W is for Mary Lou Williams. This jazz legend did it all. She taught young artists like Thelonious Monk the rich African American history of jazz. She arranged musical compositions for greats like Dizzy Gillespie. And she went on to become one of the greatest jazz pianists to ever live.

X is for **X**avier Desandre Navarre. This Frenchman was hugely influenced by African, Cuban, and Brazilian jazz rhythms. During his career, XDN joined the National Jazz Orchestra, composed for the 1998 Football World Cup, and scored the famed film, Léon: The Professional. And he's not done yet!

Y is for Lester Young. 'Prez' was so influential that a string of younger artists tried to copy his style, including the likes of Stan Getz and Charlie Parker. Young was a sly saxophonist, creative clarinetist, and famously, the hepcat who helped invent 'jive talk.' You dig, Daddy-O?

Z is for **Dizzy** Gillespie. With massive cheeks, Dizzy helped make bebop and Afro-Cuban jazz popular. His style was all surprise, suspense, and complexity— a unique sound that led to him winning several Grammys and influencing the next generation of trumpeters.

The ever-expanding legendary library

EXPLORE THESE LEGENDARY ALPHABETS & MORE AT WWW.ALPHABETLEGENDS.COM

JAZZ LEGENDS ALPHABET
www.alphabetlegends.com

Published by Alphabet Legends Pty Ltd in 2023
Created by Beck Feiner
Copyright © Alphabet Legends Pty Ltd 2023

Printed and bound in China.

9780645851519

ALPHABET LEGENDS